Impatient Purity

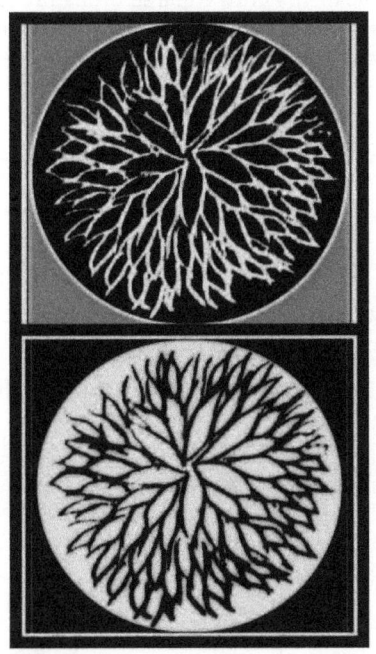

Poems, Songs, and Sustenance

Winifred Druhan

Ekstasis Multimedia
Blairstown, New Jersey

Impatient Purity Copyright ©2013 Winifred Druhan
All Rights Reserved. Printed in the United States of America.
No part of this book may be used or reproduced in any way without written permission from the publisher except in the case of brief quotations embodied in articles and reviews.
Impatient Purity/Winifred Druhan 2013
Ekstasis Multimedia, LLC/Blairstown, New Jersey:
Ekstasis Multimedia: www.booksandbrush.net

ISBN-13: 978-0615766607
ISBN-10: 0615766609

Photography, design and compilation: Marlaina Donato
Pen and ink illustrations: Winifred Druhan
Author photo: Albert Davis
All content Copyright ©1962-2004 Winifred Druhan

Table of contents

Foreword……..7

Part 1: philosophy…….9

Part 2: poems……..57

Part 3: lyrics……..86

Part 4: prose……112

About Winifred Druhan…….121

I dedicate this book to the collective morsels of pain that brought me wisdom and pressed my creative fruit into the wine of awareness.

W.D.

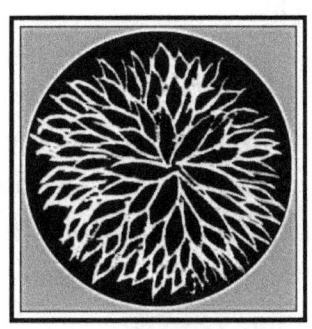

Foreword

This little book you hold in your hands reflects the individual soul of its author, yet like most heartfelt art, its quiet wisdom, private pain, human joy, and spiritual longing is universal.

Preparing a manuscript for publication is a tedious task; preparing the work of someone now deceased and close to your heart can be even more challenging. Winifred Druhan was a poet, singer-songwriter, casual philosopher, and mystic. She was also my mother. I was blessed to be raised by a woman who filled my childhood with music, poetry, and a Sufi-inspired consciousness that saw the Beloved or God even in the most miniscule.

In my youth, I struggled to understand some of my mother's deepest work, and it has taken me decades to say that I finally comprehend its many layers—layers of meaning sometimes intricately woven, each connected to a whole that is extraordinarily human yet other-worldly. Her words can undulate with dark human struggle one moment while humor and innocence can pop up like playful birds the next.

Winifred was a private woman; her body of work spans decades, yet very little of it ever saw the light of day. Despite compiling a small manuscript of quotes and having plans to illustrate it, she kept most of her thoughts on scraps of paper tucked inside her favorite books. Only after her death did I discover the true gems, many presented in this volume.

It has taken me eight years to be able to reconcile with the fact that my mother's many gifts rotted on the vine due to ill health, life circumstances, and lack of integrity in "the business." But upon close examination, her success is evident; she has left behind a living body of work that is nothing less than sustenance for the hungry spirit. Her life, in scraps and yellowed paper, has rested in my hands, and it is my honor to place it into yours, the reader's. May you be blessed with a snippet of insight, a whisper of beauty, or validation of shared human experience.

Marlaina Donato April 3, 2013

Philosophy

How can a flower that has bloomed,
gloried, and withered
envy the bud?

The body is merely a cellular cathedral.

The wages of pain should be enlightenment; pain without wages of wisdom is the toil of fools.

A destination is never behind you.

If we had the courage to be born,
we have what it takes to see this life
through.

No labor can miss the harvest unless
you look for it out of season.

First love…
the bursting forth of the first bloom
on a bush of many buds.

Your truth-

My truth-

who has the truth?

No one…everyone

Everyone's truth is truth

in his moment in time.

All self-criticism comes from loyalty to manmade ideas.

Know thyself…
Also be thyself.
Act thyself.
Answer to thyself.
Be true to thyself,
And love thyself as thy neighbor.

To receive the harvest, you first have to sacrifice the seed into the ground.

"Wasting time" is being free.

If you must be prey for the hawk, choose the hawk that feeds on you carefully; perhaps you can glean some wisdom from his belly.

When walking through the jungle, one should pick the berries of sustenance at hand, for the path ahead may be bare.

When utilized, regret
can be precaution for the future.

The tree gives up its leaves
knowing that spring
will give them back.

No one is a throw-away soul…
the Infinite Intelligence recycles.

Feeling cannot be taught,
only earned.

Love is never acquired,
only recognized.

Picking the bud in its cradle of immaturity is to not reach one's divine potential.

If living is the art of furthering the betterment of humankind, then we all should be artists.

When you play in the muck with swine you have to convince them of your worth.

We must taste every fruit in God's orchard of life, whether bitter or sweet, so we may cultivate experience to ferment our spiritual wine.

The death of the carnal mind
gives birth to Spirit.

The critic
is creativity's undertaker.

Pain is a necessary discipline that forces faith in Self and inspires original thought.

If you can still admire a bird in flight, you haven't lost your wings.

Karma is re-winding the twine of experience.

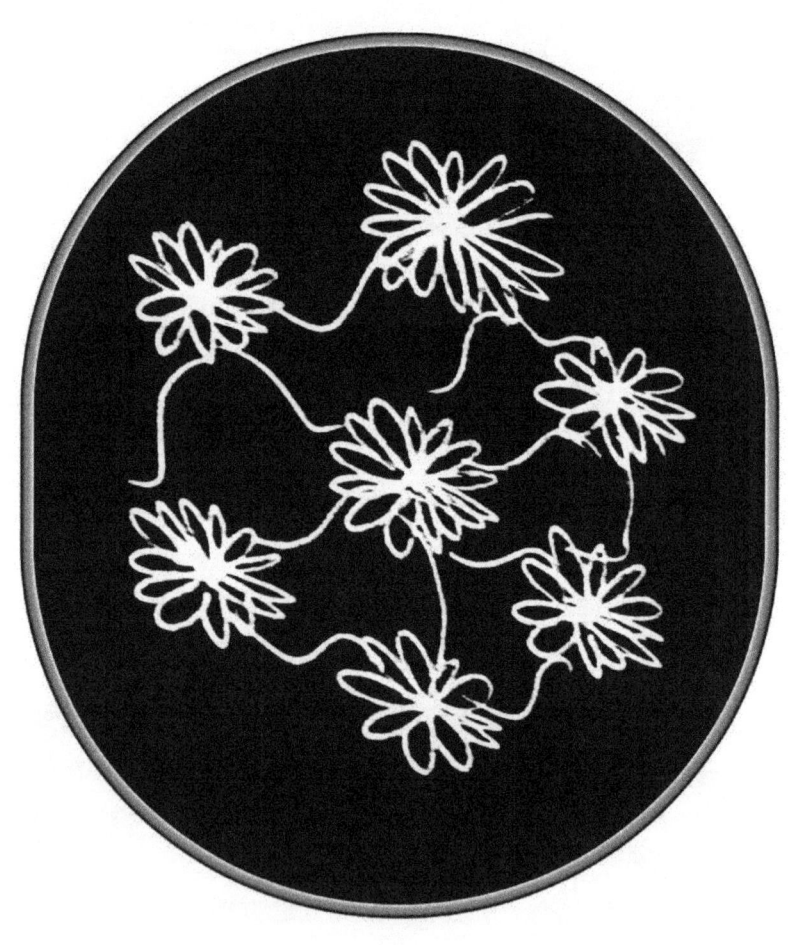

Instinct is simply the will-ess state of attunement with the Creator.

The simplicity in life is the jewel of the heavens.

Ego is the crust that imprisons the essence of the spirit.

Earth life is no more than birth-labor,
the prelude to the symphony
of God-Realization.

The scoundrel of the present age is the future's brilliant sage.

Truth is a disease greatly feared by the herd-mind.

No one has truly lived until one has been in love, found a love, and lost a love.

The true artist is an emotional alchemist transforming emotion into a manifestation of beauty.

No one can judge another person's
life by one scene in the play.

The biological marriage:
when soul mates turn into cell mates

Poems

Oddments of the Seasons

April morning sun, aqueous jewel of dew
Infant leaf, drink anew

Sleepy flower, unfold thy petals for the dawn
Renew thy faith and kiss the morn

Lone, lonely cricket
End of summer's tired song
Close your eyes, winter's long

Autumn tree ornate in crimson shroud
How proud
Before thy naked sleep

Young Pain

Young pain can rip death by the roots
And sow again.
Young pain can find hope in promise
And wait in vain.
Young pain can squander.
Young pain can wonder.
Young pain can make itself
Known like thunder.
Young pain can dream earthly dreams,
Young pain can start new streams,
But young pain can run out of time,
Never knowing that old pain is divine.

Age of Kali

Magnificent conception- world peace
Gestation period, one of chaos
Two forces at war,
Positive and negative
The convinced against the
unconvinced

I hear the clock in heaven's tower
It chimes the eleventh hour
Eyes of flesh, hearts of stone
Even kings shall die alone

The crowd disperses
One by one
The colored lights flicker out
The night is upon us, the lonely night
Is upon us
Don't reach out, reach in.

Stone

When one lover shuts his eyes,
One lover walks alone;
One lover cries
To a heart turned to stone.
When one lover cries,
A beggar's tears
Buy a beggar's throne.

The Cold One

Tiny, cold bird
Fluttering wings
Against my windowpane,
Do you look for warmth from me?
Or should I envy *you*
With your God-centered
consciousness?
I think…I am the cold one!

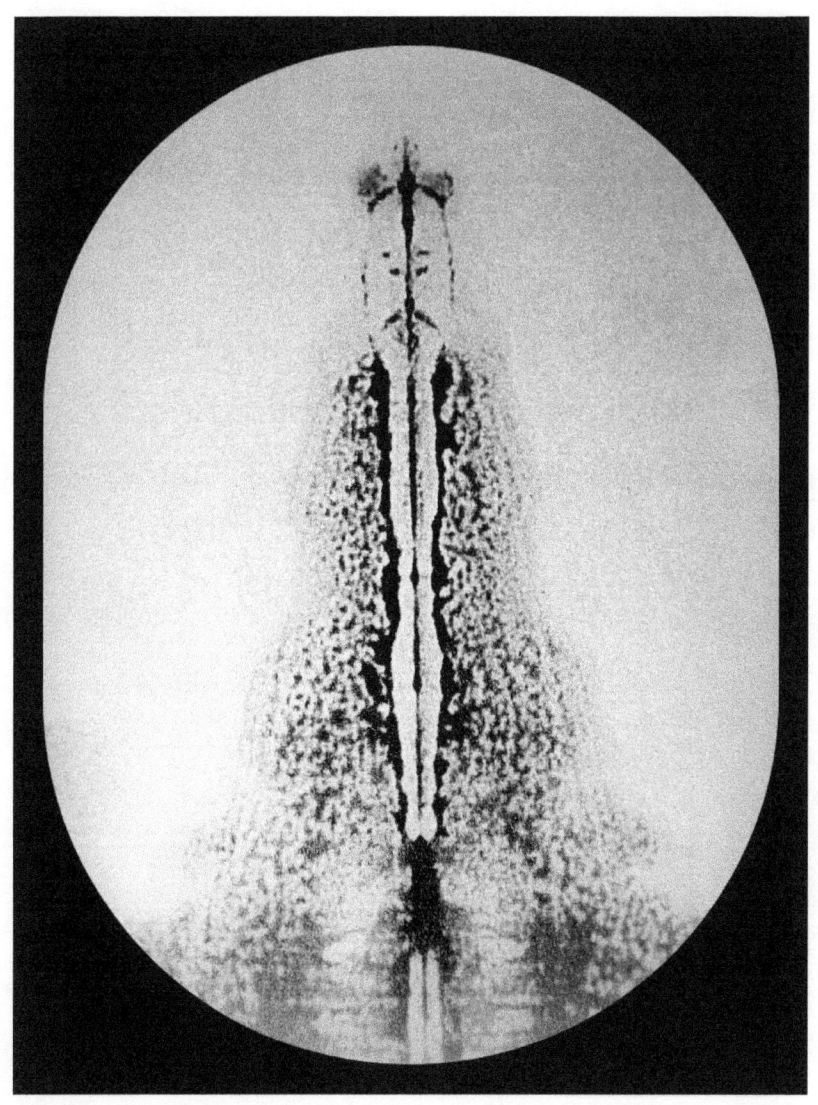

Pearl

I fling the door of darkness wide;
My spirit enters in
To where
Wisdom and the masters hide
From the maze of earth and din.
I walked my arid mile of need;
I scrambled for the chaff.
As I hold the golden pearl of peace,
I laugh.
I laugh.
I laugh.

Teacup

My father was frustration,
My mother pain.
Born a goldfish in a teacup
Dependent on rain,
My fare were the crumbs, thrown by
the few;
Oh, to glimpse a rose or two!
…To outgrow the wisdom this cup
Can afford,
Yet unable to break the umbilical
cord.
Are there rivers
That flow to oceans blue?
Should my cup runneth over,
Would I find this true?
Are there gods of freedom, gods of
Bliss
When one's vision is vast
Yet the chains persist?

Perhaps,
There will be a heavenly shore
On which to run
And swim no more.

New Wine

Lean toward my sun, beloved,
Hear only my song…
Grow in spirit
To my idea of perfection.
Lean toward *my* sun, beloved,
Hear only *my* song…
Be my mirror so *I* may shine.
Come intoxicate me
With love's new wine.

Impatient Purity

Simple son of earth
Entombed in a carcass of wants, of Greed,
Ensnarled by the nets of the deep
While karmic tides prolong the sleep.
Brilliant son of truth,
Eons of pain away,
Forever the role of the sleuth
To find a space to play.
Eyes everywhere looking for flaws;
Helping hands turn into claws.
Egoic barnacles anchor us fast,
And the shedding is painful
'Til the last.
Hypnotic hook, thy bait I swallow…
Safe, little net, I wallow, I wallow.
Oh beast, I feel thy weight…
My blood, thy passion?
My death, thy fate?

Futility

A bird with no place to land
Circling, endlessly circling
No heaven in this sky
No heaven
No earth
No rest, no rest
Just tired wings, tired wings
Hold out, tired wings, hold out

To the Anonymous Poet

Who are you, dear soul, who reaches
From the grave with pen in hand
And steers my sinking vessel
So I may understand?
Who are you, with words
That soothe the defeated heart
And slay the ghosts of doubt?
Because of you,
Another night, another day
My hopes are not without.
Where would wanting creatures be
If not for you to help us see?
No fame is spread, no name is signed;
Your soul in words,
Lives on through time.

Cocoon

Oh, flesh infirm
You house my wings.
If not for this mortal cocoon,
My soul could soar,
A butterfly to heaven's door.

Love's Destiny

Child of the Infinite,
I would know you anywhere.
Love has a way of seeking
'Til it finds a mated pair.
We were groping in the dark
'Til we saw each other's light,
And when soul met soul,
Love chased away the night.

Gestation

Your heart beat in the rhythm
Of my heartbeat,
I nourished your body with my own.
You saw through my eyes
Until your new eyes could see.
Miracle child of my own,
The infinite cosmos counted the days,
Partners we,
In love's creation...
Nestled in the silence of expectancy
Awaiting this sacred duration.

And now I hear your voice
And see your form clothed
In the rags of earth;
Finite angel, gracing my life,
May God give me the strength
And the worth.

Transience

Precious hour,
A symphony of peace…
But as the fragile flower,
All things born of time must cease.

Search

The most beautiful talent
Is hearing love's call,
A talent the most humble can wear,
For life is a search without an end,
A search for something
Just around the bend,
A search for something
We know not where
Never hearing God's whisper,
"It is here…it is here."

Truth

Truth must trod
Through mud and sod,
But how a lie
Can fly, my God!
Truth, why do you trudge on,
Weathered one,
With a road so long
And the ears so few?
"I must go on," Truth says,
"And on and on.
I have an eternal job to do."

A Prayer

Oh Lord, don't let me hear
That little voice of doubt and fear,
That little voice that tries to say
That You're not here to light my way.
Make me strong so I can tide
The voices of vanity, ego, and pride,
The voice that says to look away
If someone needs my help today.
While I'm a guest upon Your earth
And keeper of Your land,
Please help me fill my cup of worth
And let me be Your helping hand.

The Lover

Bursting with the eager fruit
Of savored love,
The young heart
Is picked and imprisoned,
Tasted and eaten,
Until the last sweet morsel is given.
Without reciprocation, the seeds of
The fruit wither and die
As the unseeded womb.
With an empty cup of passion,
The door of splendor opens wide,
And the cocoon of willing bonds
Breaks forth
With wings of proud freedom.
Oh, beautiful sky of loneliness,
I will soar with you for a fortnight,
'Til the heart swells once again
With foolish blindness
And tries once more.

The Soul

Out of the mist,
The soul walks with a staff.
The eyes have seen the night
And the pools of pain
In its caverns of woe.
Old as the mountains,
Young as the embryo,
The soul walks through
The fog of indifference
Guided by a circle of light
Upon the brow,
A flame sure to conquer the winds
Along the way.
Oh, mighty spirit, Heaven and Hell
Are the same to you;
Summer and winter are one,
All one on the road to Home.
Wrap tightly the cloak of faith,
For the way is cold.

Do not search for shoes
When you were given wings.

The Christmas Tree

Sad, little tree
Your beauty is spent,
And you long for rest.
Your moment is gone.
Return to the earth's fertile breast;
You must go on.
Tired, little tree,
You droop and sag.
We keep you here with memories dear.
We'll take you down and let you go;
You gave your life for us, we know.
Next time around,
Perhaps on a summer day,
As a butterfly, you will pass our way,
And we will smile
Because we will have found
You're no longer rooted to the ground.

The Nobody Blues

Fill your gut, drink your fill.
Go to bed, take your pill.
Take a walk, feel the cold cement.
Smell the fumes, pay the rent.
Manicure the blistered hands.
Wipe the sweat, put on the fans.
Shovel the snow, slip on the ice.
Try to escape
'Til your brain's in a vice.
Take a vacation, get a disease
Then you won't feel guilty
For having some ease.
Maybe tomorrow you can live today-
Your day off could fall
On a sunny day!

Selected Lyrics

INDECISION

I teeter on the edge of indecision
My divided
aching heart
Makes my footing unsure
Compassion and passion
blind my vision
Love is pain
such pain, when love is pure
To whom do I belong?
my old love or the new?
I have to choose but one,
but I've pledged my soul to two
The evening crystal stars
sketch my new lover's face
The constant morning sun
just reminds me of my place
I teeter on the edge of indecision
Love is pain
such pain, when love is pure

WITHOUT RESERVATION

Without reservation
without hesitation
I love you
I love you
Without thoughts of tomorrow
without fear we can borrow
I need you
I need you

My spirit breaks the bonds of flesh
and soars the heavens high
and sees a world no mortal sees
when I behold my beloved's eyes

Complete communication
completed destination
My search is through
My Love, there's you

NAKED SOUL

Paint peels and metals rust
Man dies and turns to dust
How clothed we are with gold,
how cold
the naked soul
Love knows no shade of skin
'cause love only dwells within
We say that love is free
yet give it miserly
We search for God
in temples of stone
when God is found
in man alone
We pray to save a mortal skin
yet won't forgive our neighbor's sin
Paint peels and metals rust
Man dies and turns to dust
How clothed we are with gold
how cold
the naked soul

WHEN YOU WALKED INTO MY LIFE

When you walked into my life
my life walked into your hands
I couldn't even hear your name…
I had a vision of two wedding bands
When you said "how do you do?"
I heard you saying, "I do."
You took my hand
I couldn't stand
and that's how my life began
Sometimes it happens this way
Once in a million that's true
I'll always remember the day
when I first fell in love with you
When you walked into my life
something inside me just knew
When we walk out of this life
I'll walk out right beside you

SEA STARS

Elusive little sea stars
Moonlight
makes you twinkle on the deep
Inducive little sea stars
Like love, you're always out of reach
Like love, you're never mine to keep
Their silvery ballet
like love, can blind the eye
and when the night is gray,
like love, can dance away
Intriguing little sea stars
Your luster only makes me weep
Deceiving little sea stars
Like love, you're never mine to keep
Like love, you're never mine to keep

OLD LOVES

Where do old loves go, oh Lord,
where do they go when they're dead?
Where do old dreams dream, oh Lord,
where do they lay their heads?
There must be a place
where they go to die,
a place where all lovers cry
Where do old loves go, oh Lord,
where do they go when they're gone?
Where do old dreams dream, oh Lord,
do they keep dreaming on?
Love is such a fragile thing,
it can wither and die
like time withers spring
Where do old loves go, oh Lord,
where does love go when it dies?
Where do old dreams dream, oh Lord,
where do they close their eyes?

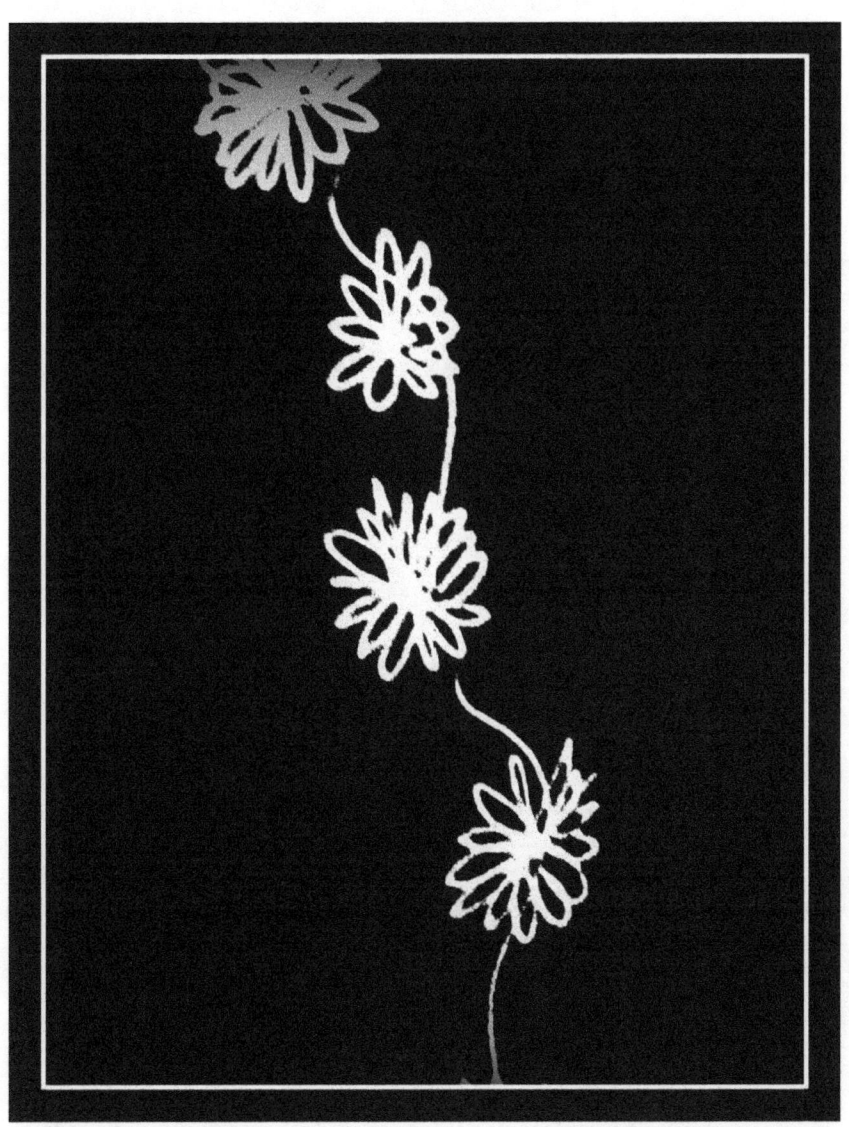

WHEN THERE'S NO LOVE AT ALL

There comes a time
in the seasons of love
when love like the rose
unfolds just to die
You just can't see
that love's flower is gone
our time has come
love's season is done
You'll never miss the sunshine
'til the shadows fall
You'll never miss my love
'til there's no love at all
There's a time for us all
You'll never miss a blue sky
'til the raindrops fall
and they're going to fall
I have given my all
I always knew I was loving for two
and when I'm through

I know just what you'll do…
You'll never miss the sunshine
'til the shadows fall
and they're going to fall
when there's no love at all

EVERYTHING CHANGES

Pretty clouds play
and the wind blows them away
Everything changes
from day to day
A flower blooms and a flower dies
Everything changes
like the love in your eyes
You've given to me
all your love when our skies were gray
you were faithful and true
yes, we shared all the way
Now you want me to say,
"Take your love and we'll call our love
a day."
A river flows
Birds build new nests ev'ry spring
Everything changes
I guess even love's a seasonal thing
Take your new love and go
if you're sure she's your everything

YOU DON'T HAVE TO BE ALONE TO BE ALONE

You don't have to be alone
to be alone
You don't have to be alone to cry
You don't have to wear a sign,
"I'm all alone"
Lovers all know when you walk by
You don't have to say,
"I hurt" to feel the pain
It doesn't show when Fate blows
out the flame
My intuition says your heart left
home
I don't have to be alone
to be alone.

MOVE THIS MOUNTAIN

We've tried and tried
each earthly way
to bridge the gap to love
but stone by stone
and hurt by hurt
a wall of hate has grown
We find we cannot penetrate
this mountain in between
I'm praying for a miracle
to make our pastures green
Oh, move this mountain,
oh Lord, I pray
Oh move this mountain of hate today
They say that faith can move
mountains right away
Oh move this mountain of hate today
We never dreamed each little spat
could make this mountain grow
but now we're sitting on the top and
lookin' where to go

If we could learn from past mistakes
our future would be fine
Some people say to look ahead
but I say look behind

CURTAIN OF DARKNESS

The curtain of darkness
that love can wear
The dancer only sees the stage
The light of love can blind and glare
A dance of death can be the wage
Love has no eyes for lovers to see
The way is dark
Love's a dark mystery
Love only hears the lover's voice
Love has no fear
Love has no choice
The curtain of darkness
will lift someday
The dancer then will see her way
The lights of love will no longer glare
The curtain of darkness was sweet
and fair

PRIMA DONNA SUNSHINE

Share your light,
Prima Donna Sunshine
What you are, always be what you are
Just shine for me
Prima Donna Sunshine
always free
I'll always let you be free
Don't let the world
don't let them try to make you over
Don't let the world
try to make you what
they want you to be
My mystic star,
Prima Donna Sunshine
What you are
let them see what you are
Don't let the world
don't let them try to make you over
Don't let the world try to make
you something you can never be

Just shine for me,
Prima Donna Sunshine
always free,
I know your need to be free
Just shine for me,
Prima Donna Sunshine
always free

I'M A DREAMER

I'm a dreamer
And I'm looking for a dreamer
Where do I find a dreamer?
Doesn't the dreamer exist?
I'm a lover
and I'm looking for a lover
Where do I find a lover
who needs the lifetime
of love I've missed…
I've sifted the sands of humanity
looking for someone who loves like me
I've walked all the deserts of time
with a thirst for a love that's divine
a love that's exclusively mine
I'm a dreamer
and I'll always be a dreamer
Just waiting for my dreamer
who's looking for a love
that leaves all other loves behind

AND THERE'S LOVE

There's love and there's love
There's your kind of love
and there's mine
There's love and there's love
for me you don't have the right kind
for me you don't have the right kind
You want to be loved
but you don't know how to love
With me, love is strong
but to me your eyes don't belong
But to me your eyes don't belong
…a heart that is snagged,
a heart snagged on fickle thorns
A heart that is snagged, to me this
heart doesn't belong
To me this heart doesn't belong,
a heart snagged on fickle thorns
There's love and there's love
There's your kind of love and there's
mine

There's love and there's love
so please come back some other time
sometime when your eyes are all mine

THE ELEVENTH HOUR
(A World Anthem)

There's love in every woman
There's love in every man
There's love in you and me,
child of God,
there's love in every land,
every land
There are storm clouds coming,
and the clouds are forming fast,
child of God,
hear the warning
or this storm could be the last
be our last
It's the world's eleventh hour
We can no longer stand alone
Love is a force, a source of power
like we've never known,
ever known
These few precious hours
we must choose to love or die

child of God,
hear the warning
We must choose to love or die,
love or die
It's the world's eleventh hour
We can no longer stand alone
Love is a force, a source of power
like we've never known,
ever known
forever known

HOW LONG IS FOREVER

How long is forever?
Can it be a day or two?
How long can forever be?
Is it just 'til love is through?
How long is for always?
Is it just a dreamtime long?
Isn't for always forever?
or maybe I'm wrong...
The forevers that you promised away
you can never hope to pay
Oh yes the time will come for me
when I'll be just a memory
How long is forever?
Is it worth a broken heart?
Your forevers aren't eternal
but I'm game...
When do we start?

WEEDS

On your way to the top
take a good look around
Keep your spirits on high
Keep your feet on the ground
for we all have a dream
in this world to fulfill
but we also have a garden to till
so don't let your spiritual garden have
weeds
let it be flowered with love and good
deeds
While fitting the key
in the lock of your goal
remember that we only leave
with a soul
remember that we have a short time
to sow
hey there mister, how does your
garden grow?

So don't let your spiritual garden have weeds
let it be planted with heavenly seeds
Let it be watered with helping mankind
for that's the only harvest we leave behind

Prose

Graduation

Life is a hell-school, and at the end of the term, we receive our diplomas in pain. But sometimes, we don't learn anything at all, spending life cutting class, floating through time, and worshipping the body only to watch it decay. We grease and build it up and tear it down until the pain of it all unmasks the truth and shows us an inner self.

Pain in itself is kind; it is a teacher, a disciplinarian, the kind yet often violent knowledge-bearing parent who peels flesh from the bones to get down to the unseen treasures of soul.

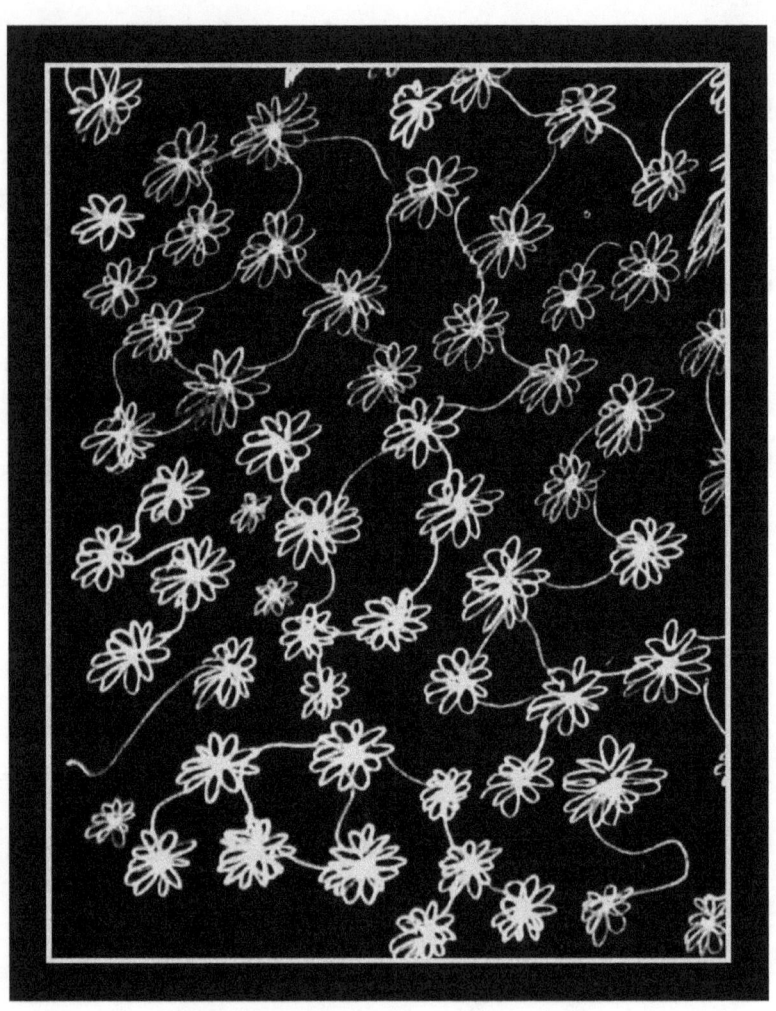

The Last Mile of Faith

The Gods have no need for earth angels, only veterans of pain who live through the snares and traps of the dark forces—the experienced guide who walks the last mile of faith and leaves a trail behind for the unaware and the vulnerable who seek a glimpse of Truth.

The Attic

The heart can be like an old attic… to keep it clean, we must open the windows and let love's sunshine fill every crevice; get rid of all the old junk that has been stored- old hurts, hate, and prejudice; sweep it out with happiness, thankfulness, humility, and store only good deeds and loving thoughts so someday the attic can be opened and remembered someday by those we love.

...Awaken tired, earthly eyes...
the jewels are there for us to see,
    the jewels of our eternity...

Winifred Druhan

Winifred Druhan (1927-2005) was born in Brooklyn, New York and managed health food stores in New York City until the early 1960s. She and her husband Tom abandoned urban living to build a house and a new life in rural Pennsylvania. Winifred—or Winni as she was often called—independently studied alternative medicine, holistic arts, and metaphysics; occasionally, she offered lectures on natural health and shared her faith that embraced spiritual truth within all religions. She was a visionary who believed that we can learn something from everything, "even the tiny ant who empties a sugar bowl one grain at a time." To order her CD single The Eleventh Hour or for professional inquiries, please contact Ekstasis Multimedia at **www.booksandbrush.net**

www.ingramcontent.com/pod-product-compliance
Lightning Source LLC
Chambersburg PA
CBHW032139040426
42449CB00005B/322